Black Free Me

Black Free Me
Volume 3: Rollercoaster
Queen Billyne

To my friends and most importantly my family, may all of our dreams come true.

Preface

When initially writing the third volume of Black Free Me, what I had in mind was Therapy, because I feel like therapy is an important step when it comes to healing. I believed it was time to take my readers and myself to therapy, but then it occurred to me that I wasn't at all healing, I was stuck in a never-ending emotional rollercoaster. Happiness, joy, abandonment, love, pain, confusion, lust, heartbreak and grief. And through those emotions, I wrote, and I continue to write. I feel like I would have cheated you all if I didn't let you in to see and feel this rollercoaster.

"Seeing where you need improvement is the biggest revelation, trying to make those changes requires determination."
-Queen Billyne

It was seven o'clock on a Thursday night and I was home in bed thinking about how happy I should be, thinking about how I messed up and what I should've done. The what-ifs always seem to echo loudly when you're alone. I isolated myself from my friends again; I wonder if they've noticed, they probably don't even care. Why should they? They've got what they wanted, I gave them the best parts of me and now I'm lost and empty. I got up and walked downstairs to the kitchen and straight towards the liquor cabinet, there were three bottles of unopened wine calling out to me. *Barefoot* always did the trick. I grabbed the corkscrew and went back upstairs to my room. I shut the door and locked it. I just needed to get away. I placed the bottle of wine on the dresser and searched for my journal and pen. I felt my anxiety rising and the tears forming. I didn't want to think anymore, I didn't want to feel anymore. But it was too late; I was on the ground holding my knees to my chest, dry heaving, shaking, and crying. The walls began closing in, the room was spinning, and everything was getting dark.

I didn't know how much time had passed by; I was on the floor looking under my bed wondering did I make the right decision in my life. I got up and reached for the bottle of wine. I wonder if this is how addictions begin. I began to pace my room, how much longer until I'm satisfied? How much longer until I can finally feel free? There are too many people depending on me, too many people looking up to me. I stopped pacing and placed the wine on my desk and searched for my journal and pen.

Finally, the mint cover greeted me; I flipped through looking for the next empty page. Finally, a blank page welcomes me. I uncapped my pen and began to write, and the ink began to bleed, and these are the words I wrote that put my soul to ease.

Genesis

Unsure of where I fit in
Feeling like being black was a sin
Afraid to talk
Too terrified to walk
Couldn't get mad
Suppressed so many emotions I only felt sad
Until finally I was taught to love my skin.
Beautiful and full of melanin
Learning about all its beauty
Seeing the sun shine on us and crown us royalty
Understanding that I was black
I was able to see my community and the things that
we lacked.
I have seen the chains
I felt the pain
And still my people were afraid to teach me
Ashamed of our history.
Seeing how far we kept falling
Gave myself a new calling.
And now that it's clear
I'm glad that I'm here
To play my part
And leave a mark
In my community
And that was the Genesis
Of Black Free Me.

I embarrassed myself for you.
I hurt myself and loved you.

October 2018

Being everything you wanted me to be
But forgetting who I am
Trying more than once to leave
But running back to you like an insensible and
delusional fan
Corrupted my way of love
Because your definition was the only way
Your way or the highway
And my heart was unable to merge and yield
Now I'm stuck in a three-car collision with my heart,
mind, and soul
Damn, this love is taking its toll
But I was willing to pay
Not realizing just how much I was drained

Being everything you wanted me to be
And never succumbing to temptation
Being everything you wanted me to be
But you weren't living up to my expectations
You were everything to me
But realizing I wasn't enough
You were everything to me
How wasn't I enough?

Re-set,
      Re-adjust,
            Re-start,
                  Re-focus.

Friends

Friends don't exist
People who claim they're there
But away seem to disappear
These people I used to miss
And then it occurred to me

Who were these people?
And what does 'friend' really mean?
The definition plus their true intentions
Lead me to believe that friends
Are people that just pretend

To care
To love
To be there

In the end
It's clear to me
That I am my friend
None of you, just me.

You never love two people the same,
The person is different, the feeling is different
The love itself is different.

Love Jones

In a Sentimental Mood
Thinking about how well we go together
Like John and Duke
Mixing together like Jazz and Blues
Thinking about it who knew?
That a feeling like this
Started 'cause you flipped the script,
Went out of your element
Doing things out of the norm, causing embarrassment
 Sumthin Sumthin
About the lust we're feeling
Heat blazing inside our bodies
Mellosmoothe when you hold and touch me
You finally became the funk in my right thigh
When I realized...
I was your lady
And I'm crazy bout you baby
Like lovers do, we hit a rift
And then we split
Left, came back
And here's a fact
I will never ever, ever stop loving you
Damn, I'm back... In my sentimental mood
On this Coltrane passing Ellington
Thinking about how this love is soul food
So caught up my head is starting to spin
Because you have me so wrapped in
And I'm starting to realize this
"You always want
What you want
When you want it.
        Why is everything so urgent with you?"
Looking into your eyes

As I heard you reply
"This right here, right now,
    At this very moment is all that matters to me.
      I love you.
        And that's urgent like a muthafucka."

The universe connects the right people to each other.

I Want

The things I want
Aren't usually good for me.
The things I crave the most end up a catastrophe.
Like you,
My heart's drawn to the way you smile.
I'm here willing to go the extra mile.

Fighting for your attention
When my feelings for you have never been mentioned.
Forcing myself to keep this feeling a secret
Has me failing miserably
Because I'm craving your love desperately.
An attraction like this is obvious
But space separates us and that's what makes it
dangerous.

The things I want
Aren't usually good for me.
Because here I am thinking about you
But, the truth?
I could never have you
Because you belong to her
And usually, I wouldn't care
But that smile I like so much
Is the same smile on your face just by her touch.
Who am I to rob you of such ecstasy?
I admit this sadness that I feel is pure jealousy.

The things I want the most
Usually aren't meant for me
But this is easy to accept
Because honestly, I'm just happy we even met.

I crave the type of passion that makes me jump just out of anticipation.

Fantasy

Round three
Go deep
Out of breath
We're chest to chest
You groan
I moan.
You make
Me shake
It's not a race
But you quicken the pace.
Back scratched
Flip me over and I throw it back
You pound
And damn I love that sound
As we rhythmically connect
Our souls entwine and that's just one of the effects.
The deeper you go I get closer to the edge
Changing locations now we're off the bed
Back arched now I'm begging for more
Hearing you grunt we're almost there -
Excuse me, miss? Are you okay?
Just wanted to know if the office is this way
Out of my daze
Yes, go straight you'll see the sign clearly
Now leave me alone so I can finish this fantasy.

Ignoring the pain didn't make it disappear.

Emptiness

Trying to feel something
But in the end, felt everything.
Then again
Feeling emptiness
Trying hard to sort feelings out
Realizing enough is enough
Lying down
On this merry-go-round
Round and round
Up and down
Getting dizzy
As emotions surround me
... yet I still feel empty.

Life is a never-ending adventure,

I often lose and find myself.

Lost on My Road to Recovery

Who's gonna listen?
Whose at least gotta minute?
I just need to explain
I need to let go of all this pain.
I've never felt this low
The road to recovery is backed up
Traffic jam on Identity Ave
You know the intersection where Love Street and Pain
Blvd meet.
My mind is unable to function
Caught up in this conjunction.
Tell me, how do I get out?
Because it seems to me I've already passed this house
Feeling like a mouse
Welcome to the maze
Searching for answers
But I've been stuck here for days.

First step in self-growth is being honest with yourself.

The One That Got Away

Hey you,
Everything I did
I didn't mean to
I picked all of them
Over you
Thinking I could get you back
Now look at me, my life's off track
Chance after chance
But I did it over again.
Now I'm wondering what could've been
Well, here I am
Thinking about all those memories
And I swear, I didn't mean to leave
Here, I go making more excuses.
I'm the reason for all of your bruises
You probably don't want to hear it from me
But
I am truly sorry
Cause we could've flourished
Instead of being so malnourished
Looking up and I caught your eyes.
The light shine
Mirrors glare
Watching my reflection look back at me
Knowing it's me
Letting myself go
Ending up lost
And still willing to stay.
I was there when they all broke my heart
I was there when my self-esteem fell apart
Loving who I was and am takes a special form of art
And before I ruin this again
Let me ask

Can you please stay?
Because you're the real one that got away.

No one has ever broken your heart.
They've broken your expectations.

Subtract

How do you expect me to love you?
When I no longer love me?
I'm definitely confused.
I know you see these bruises
From the emotionally manipulative way you loved me.
Funny because you once sustained me,
Now you're causing my insanity.
I can't say I hate you
Because you taught me to love.
I can't say I love you
And that's not something I'm proud of.
I can't love you
Because of the way you broke me.
Dismantled my self-esteem
Made me really believe
That I wasn't worthy?
I need to be without you,
Love without you,
Be me without you.
You're beginning to stifle me
And I don't want to be mean
But... I can only grow ...
Without you.

Understand what you're worth, cherish the value. Never give a discount and remember your loveyou're your time are never on sale.

What Can You Bring to the Table?

Don't come over here asking me what can I bring to
the table
When I'm the utensils you need to eat.
Without me, you'd succumb to savagery.
The napkins you need to be clean.
Without me, you'd end up messy.
The salt and pepper you use when you feel something
is lacking.
Adding the necessary spice to your life without me
you'd be slacking.
I am the table cloth that protects the table from any
stains.
Other than your insecurities and pain
What can you bring?

Life isn't meant to be gone through alone,
Yet I can't find anyone who understands me.

Rollercoaster

Teacups represent me currently
And I'm sure I'm in Disney,
Spinning trying to grasp my conscience
As everyone around laughs with glee.
Spinning
Spinning
Spinning
Now I'm dizzy
Realizing I couldn't see
Stumbled into my mind's own misery.
Mind exploding like a Volcano at Bay
Unaware that I was drowning
Emotions still swirling
Emotions still going.
Hit by reality now I'm stuck
Just my luck.
I'm down again
In so much pain
One minute I'm sad
Then next minute mad.
Can't recall when I'm happy
But once I am, I'm down feeling nasty
Cause I can't control my emotions
Yelling to my mind to stop the commotion.
Like the *Drop* at the Youth Fair
Hit with a wave of shock, I'm gasping for air.
This ride is getting too crazy
I'm crying for my sanity
Up
Down
Finally stopping
Yet I can't get down.
Panic arises as I look around

The ride starts again
Clawing at my chest for the safety belts to come off me
Cause I rather fall and die than be faced with this
misery.

To not experience love means to not have lived.

Famished

Like a wine glass before dinner,
Baby, I'm empty.
And I'm waiting here for you to unfold before me.
Pop the cork and pour it into me.
The first drop always so refreshing
Let me clear my throat and admit.

You're the one that I crave
Too deep into you my heart's in a 6-foot grave.
The cause of it all is because
I'm an addict of your love
Dependent on your very touch
Desperate for your time
Demanding your affection

Wanting your undivided attention
I need you.
I already sense myself clinging to you.
Be honest and tell the truth
Are you into me like I'm into you?
Jumping into this quicker than a kid at a swimming
pool.

No lifeguard to save me
Guess who's drowning?
Me.
Too blinded by my own wants and needs.
Ignoring the signs
Caused my heart's demise.
Falling for you
Broke me into pieces.
Picking myself back up is exactly what I needed.

The simplest thing makes even the most complicated person happy.

Reassurance

The littlest gestures can leave a lasting impression.
Truth be told baby, I have some questions,
When you held my hand before I fell asleep
Was that your way of saying you had me?
The way you smile when you see me,
Is that real babe? Do I make you happy?
I know my questions may cause annoyance.
I'm just a woman who needs a little reassurance.

If it weren't for musicians and their experiences we would all go through life alone.

Sade

You and I share
A connection so rare
A love so different if spoken
Everything around us becomes broken
The Sweetest Taboo.
If I lost this love, I'd probably die without you
And I did 'cause you left
And I wept.
But as a *Soldier A Love* I continued to fight
Fighting to bring you back to the light
You were fighting against me, but this love is *Stronger Than Pride*.
I know it because we've both cried
Even though we both hid it and lied.
Here I am still trying to be *By Your Side.*
Honestly, is it a crime?
That through all the bullshit I still think about you all the time.
Is It a Crime?
That I want you
And I want you to want me too
Trying my hardest to *Hang on to Your Love*
But it was something that I almost lost a grip of
Even though the pain was tearing me apart
I could never *Turn My Back On You*
In the end, I realized
The real reason why I tried
Was because
This is *No Ordinary Love.*

Life situations cause pain,
learn from it, make peace with it and move on.

Feelings

I don't mean to Ella Mai it
But this is something that I'm way too deep in.
My feelings... are offensive
I'm no longer allowed to be upset.
It ruins the mood, apparently to them

I'm no longer allowed to be mad
"You're so emotional".
Wouldn't you prefer me to be in tune with my emotions
Instead of being a rock eroding by the crash of the
ocean.

Now all of my emotions are suppressed.
Congratulations friends, guess what?
I'm depressed.
According to you, I'm always complaining.
I can't be that strong friend anymore.
The one that is always happy and playing.
It's draining...

This relationship is beginning to strain me,
Taking up all of my energy.
And like a tumor in the operation room.
You're killing me so you must be removed.

Now as I detach from you
I am beginning to build something new.
A place where my emotions aren't neglected.
A place where I'm truly free and my feelings respected.

*The worst battle I ever fought was between
what I knew and what I felt.*

Game Over

Detoxing my soul
You're so toxic, my heart created this hole
Find someone else to destroy
Find another heart that's a toy.
I'm leaving and never coming back
No need to block you boo, I'm gone this time it isn't an
act.

Every love you experience in life will leave a lasting impression.

Ruin Ya Life

When I say...
Let me ruin ya life
I mean in the most passionate way.
So much passion that I leave my footprints in your
brain.
That's one small step for love
And another step for Baee
Dancing and making love to your temporal lobe
Caught up in bliss
And the way we kiss
Gentle tugging on your lips
Now all you do is think of me.
Open your eyes baby it's only a memory.

Let me ruin ya life
And when we get too comfortable
And I think we're in too deep
I'll have no choice but to leave
Leaving nothing but sweet memories.

Losing someone isn't the worst part of love.
Losing yourself is.

You

You took a piece of me.
Making it seem like you were my missing link
But instead, you left and took a part of me.
Now I'm supposed to act like you never meant a thing
to me.
Lie to everyone like my heart's not screaming in agony.
Lie because I was stupid and dumber than naive.
Lie because no one needs to know that the queen
bleeds.

Started distancing myself from people who made it seem like I was difficult to love.

Jigsaw

Let's play a game
Let's call this game; society versus me.
A game where I try to fit in
Knowing that the pieces could never conform no
matter how hard I try to force them in.

Starting with the edges...
The parts everyone is able to see.
Like this smile that easily deceives
These eyes that often lie to you, but tell the truth only
to me.
This laugh that masks the pain
A laugh that lets you believe me when I make any
claim.

Like when I yell, "Girl, fuck him"
Not knowing he was the only person who knew and
understood my name.
A man that made me see the sun in any rain
Or when I say "I'm tired"
... my favorite lie...
That's when deep inside I'm tired of life.

A mini Ledisi, these are the small pieces of me.
This game does get crazy
When you get to know me.
Distorted pieces
Everyone wants to solve it
Deep down you know we should dispose of it.
A puzzle not worth being solved
A game where no one should ever get involved.
A game where it's society versus me.

*Life doesn't give you what you want...
it gives you what you deserve.*

2020

This year changed me
Challenged my mind
Went to war and battled my soul
Found parts of me I forgot existed
Discovered parts of me I manifested
I am more than I expected
I found it.
I found her.
I found me.

CPSIA information can be obtained
at www.ICGtesting.com
Printed in the USA
BVHW081448190722
642490BV00012B/800

9 781737 078401